For sweet baby

_____

From

_____

On this day

_____

Birthdate

Weight

Length

Snips & Snails

Illustrated by Becky Kelly

Written by Patrick Regan

**Andrews McMeel
Publishing**

Kansas City

www.beckykelly.com

03 04 05 06 07 EPB 10 9 8 7 6 5 4 3 2 1

ISBN: 0-7407-3910-7

Illustrations by Becky Kelly
Design by Stephanie R. Farley
Edited by Polly Blair
Production by Elizabeth Nuelle

for daniel–
whose spark
lights up
a thousand stars.
bk

Snips & Snails

When a sweet baby boy
Bounces into the world,
A lifetime of fun's just begun.

With a cry and a coo
He makes his debut . . .

And announces the rise of the son.

Face furrowed but fair,
Skin soft as a prayer . . .

Wee fingers wrap tightly 'round yours . . .

Little legs churn the air . . .

While eyes keen and aware
search a world he can't wait to explore.

They say snips and snails
And puppy dog tails
Help to make a boy hearty and hale . . .

But there's much more to add
For a well-rounded lad . . .

Whose ship's just beginning to sail.

A sprinkle of sunshine
Has made his eyes twinkle
And added a blush to his cheek.

A dash of ambition
And pinch of adventure . . .

Will make his dreams rare and unique.

A spoonful of silly,
Mixed lightly with mischief,
Will keep life from growing mundane . . .

While a teaspoon of quiet
And a cup of good sense
will ensure that his parents stay sane.

Add a measure of faith . . .

And belief in himself,
Leaving room for a lifetime of joy . . .

Then to all the above,
Add unlimited love—

That's how you make one little boy.